W9-AVC-293

MATERIALS THAT MATTER

METALS

Neil Morris

amicus

Published by Amicus
P.O. Box 1329
Mankato, MN 56002

Printed in the United States of America,
at Corporate Graphics in North Mankato, Minnesota

          Library of Congress Cataloging-in-Publication Data
Morris, Neil, 1946-
  Metals / by Neil Morris.
      p. cm. -- (Materials that matter)
  Includes index.
  Summary: "Discusses metals as a material, including historical uses, current uses,
  mining and manufacturing, and recycling"--Provided by publisher.
  ISBN 978-1-60753-066-4 (library binding)
  1. Metals--Juvenile literature. I. Title.
  TA459.M557 2011
  620.1'6--dc22

                                                        2009029797

Created by Appleseed Editions Ltd.
Designed by Helen James
Edited by Mary-Jane Wilkins
Artwork by Graham Rosewarne
Picture research by Su Alexander

Photograph acknowledgements
page 4 Mamoru Nagai/Amanaimages/Corbis; 5 Jose Manuel Sanchis Calvete/Corbis;
6 Gianni Dagli Orti/Corbis; 7 AFP/Getty Images; 8 Martyn Goddard/Corbis; 9 North Wind
Picture Archives/Alamy; 10 Txema Fernandez/epa/Corbis; 11 Corbis; 12 Robert Harding
World Imagery/Corbis; 14 James L Amos/Corbis; 15 Hussenot/PhotoCuisine/Corbis; 16 Fred
Prouser/Reuters/Corbis; 18 Paul A Souders/Corbis; 20 Dave G Houser/Corbis; 21 Gunta Marx
Photography/Corbis; 22 Joseph Sohm/Visions of America/Corbis; 23 Gideon Mendel/Corbis;
24 Tompiodesign.com/Alamy; 25 Jose Fuste Raga/Corbis; 26 Steve Crise/Transtock/Corbis;
27 Amit Dave/Reuters/Corbis; 28 Boris Roessler/dpa/Corbis; 29 Denis Scott/Corbis
Front cover Fred Prouser/Reuters/Corbis

DAD0041
32010

9 8 7 6 5 4 3 2 1

Contents

What Are Metals?

We see metal every day in cars, bicycle frames, knives, forks, and cans. Metals are chemical **elements**, which means that they can't be broken down into other substances. More than three-quarters of all the Earth's elements are metals.

Most factory parts and machines are made of metal. These iron and steel pipes and walkways are strong and reliable.

We find metals in Earth's crust. There are about 80 metals all together, which form about a quarter of the materials in the crust. The best known are useful metals such as aluminum, copper, and iron, or **precious metals**, such as gold, platinum, and silver. Other lesser known metals are beryllium (which is used as a lightweight construction material), niobium (used in steel **alloys**), and technetium (a **radioactive** element).

Where Do Metals Come From?

Miners find some precious metals in a pure state—not mixed up with other elements. But most metallic elements are found in combinations with other elements called **compounds**. These are minerals, and we find them in rocks. Minerals that contain valuable metal are called **ores**. We find all the most common metals in ores, and they have different names. For example, aluminum comes mainly from an ore called bauxite. Iron comes from hematite, and tin comes from cassiterite.

Recognizing Metals

Metals have several things in common, called properties. If you want to find out whether something is metal, here are some questions to ask about it. First, is it solid? Metals are solid at room temperature, not liquid or a gas. Mercury is one exception. It is liquid and runny at room temperature. Second, does it reflect light? Most metals

USE THEM AGAIN AND AGAIN

Many metals can be used again and again (see pages 24–27). Every time we recycle metals, we help the environment. For example, we save a huge amount of energy when we recycle metals to make new metal.

Recycled Metal	Percentage of Energy Saved
aluminum	95
copper	85
steel	68
lead	60
zinc	60

reflect light with a metallic shine, especially when we polish them. Third, can it be hammered without breaking? We can shape metals in this way, which means that they are **malleable**. Another thing we can do is stretch them into thin wires. We say that they are **ductile**. Finally, does heat pass through it? Metals are good conductors of heat and electricity. One more characteristic of metals is their color—most are gray, though there are exceptions, such as copper which is red.

This rock is a chunk of iron ore called hematite.

Material Times

The Stone Age, Bronze Age, and Iron Age are times in history named after the materials that prehistoric people of each era used to make tools. The Stone Age was the earliest period in human history, before people started using metals.

Some historians add another age after the Stone Age, because the first metal prehistoric people used was copper. The Copper Age began about 10,000 years ago in Anatolia and Mesopotamia (modern Turkey and Iraq), when people found nuggets of pure copper. They hammered these into simple pins and rings. By about 5000 BC, people had learned how to get copper from ores that they dug from the ground. This process is called **smelting** (see right). Once people had learned how to smelt copper, they used it to make ornaments, tools, and weapons. The ancient Egyptians were also mining and smelting copper by about 3500 BC.

Combining with Tin

Around 3500 BC, people in Mesopotamia started mixing tin with copper to make a new metal called bronze. This alloy is harder and more durable (lasts longer) than copper. This was the beginning of the Bronze Age, which began at different times in various parts of the world. In ancient China, workers began using bronze about 2,000 years later than in Mesopotamia.

Into the Iron Age

Around 1500–1000 BC the metalworkers of Anatolia replaced bronze with iron. They did this because iron ore was easier to find and mine than copper or tin. Metalworkers could

This copper statue of the ancient Egyptian pharaoh Pepy I was made more than 4,000 years ago.

The remains of this Bronze Age village were discovered near Naples, Italy, in 2001. Ash from a volcanic eruption buried the huts and pots around 1650 BC.

SEPARATING METAL FROM ORE

Smelting allowed people to take copper, tin, and iron ore and separate the metal from the rock. To do this, they heated the ore to a very high temperature in a **furnace**. The furnace was a hole in the ground covered by stone slabs. The ore was smashed into rubble, mixed with charcoal, and heated over a very hot fire. The fire melted the ore and the metal sank to the bottom. Metalworkers could then reheat the metal and hammer it into shape.

RECYCLE RECYCLE RECYCLE

THE FIRST RECYCLERS?

In the first century AD, the Roman historian Pliny the Elder wrote that Roman metalworkers were reusing scrap copper and bronze. As they conquered new territories to expand their empire, the ancient Romans tore down metal statues and shipped them to the port of Brundisium (modern Brindisi in Italy). There they melted down the metal and recast it as armor, weapons, or new statues.

also harden iron by plunging the hot metal into water. Iron tools quickly spread through Asia and Europe. Toolmakers found it so useful that ancient Greek writers such as Homer referred to it as a precious metal.

Metals and Machines

The Industrial Revolution of the eighteenth and nineteenth centuries began in Britain. The first factories were built and machines started to mass-produce all sorts of goods that had been made by hand. Iron was a vital material during this time.

Some historians say that the Industrial Revolution started in 1709, when the English ironmaker Abraham Darby (1678–1717) converted a furnace to smelt iron by burning **coke**. Before then, metalworkers had used charcoal as fuel, which was more expensive and more difficult to obtain. Darby's family continued to improve iron and find new uses for it.

Brunel's iron steamship, the Great Britain, *is now a museum in the docks at Bristol.*

Bridges, Rails, and Ships

Abraham Darby's son, Abraham Darby II (1711–63) improved the quality of the company's iron. Grandson Abraham Darby III (1750–91) became even more famous. He built the world's first cast-iron bridge, which opened in 1779. It still stands today, spanning 98 feet (30 m) across the Severn River in western England.

Twenty-five years later, the engineer Richard Trevithick (1771–1833) ran a steam locomotive on rails in an ironworks. The combination of steam and iron—the power of boiling water and the strength and usefulness of the metal—changed the industrial world. In 1843, engineer Isambard Kingdom Brunel (1806–59) designed and built the world's first propeller-driven iron steamship, the *Great Britain*.

Converting to Steel

During the 1850s, British engineer Henry Bessemer (1813–98) invented a new process for converting iron into harder, stronger steel. Until then steel had been rare, because it was difficult and expensive to make. Bessemer's new process poured molten iron from a furnace into a large egg-shaped container called a converter. Air was blown into the container, which was lined with limestone or clay. The heat formed slag from **impurities** in the iron and removed some of the carbon in the metal. The molten steel was poured out by tipping the converter. This new process halved the price of steel.

USING IRON

Iron was useful for making machines (which made other things) as well as metal objects. The molten iron that came from a furnace was known as pig iron. This could be used by blacksmiths and metalworkers to make wrought iron. They reheated the iron and **forged** (or hammered) it into shape. In foundries, workers turned the pig iron into cast-iron objects. First they remelted the iron, then they cast (or poured) it into **molds** to shape it. Cast iron could be mass-produced, and it was the most important building material until steel replaced it.

This illustration from the 1880s shows molten iron being poured into a Bessemer converter in Pittsburgh, Pennsylvania.

How We Use Modern Metals

Since the nineteenth century, metalworkers and industrialists have found ways of using many more metals. Some, such as aluminum, were new metals. Others, such as tin, had been known for centuries but became useful in new ways. The first tin cans for storing food were made in the 1800s. They were called tin cans, but they were actually made of tin-plated steel.

Discovering Aluminum

In 1825, Danish scientist Hans Christian Oersted (1777–1851) produced the first aluminum from aluminum oxide. Today we get this metal from the ore bauxite. Aluminum is very light and weighs just a third as much as steel. It does not rust and can be made stronger by mixing it with small amounts of copper, magnesium, or zinc. It is perfect for all sorts of uses, from aluminum foil to drink cans. In the early twentieth century, American inventor Elwood Haynes (1857–1925) started using aluminum in car engines. Haynes also discovered stainless steel.

Radioactive Metals

In 1896, the French physicist Antoine Henri Becquerel (1852–1908) studied the metal uranium. He discovered that invisible rays coming from a lump of uranium ore changed

Titanium panels cover the Guggenheim Museum in Bilbao, Spain. The sculpture of a giant spider is made of bronze and steel.

Nuclear plants turn powdered uranium into metal discs, like this one. The radioactive powder is made from uranium ore, which is mined from underground.

a photographic plate in the same way as X-rays. The uranium was giving off energy, and Becquerel had discovered radioactivity.

Two years later, Polish-born scientist Marie Curie (1867–1934) and her French husband Pierre Curie (1859–1906) found other radioactive metals. They named them polonium (after Marie's homeland) and radium (from the word ray). Becquerel and the Curies jointly won the Nobel Prize for physics in 1903 for these discoveries.

Making Nuclear Energy

Nuclear power comes from the energy stored inside tiny particles called **atoms**. Some metallic elements, such as uranium, have unstable atoms. This means the central **nucleus** of their atoms can break apart, and when they do, they give off huge amounts of energy. We produce nuclear power by breaking nuclei apart, releasing heat energy that boils water and creates steam. The steam then drives an electric **generator**.

Light and Strong

Titanium was first made in large quantities in 1948. It is difficult and expensive to separate this light, strong, stainless metal from its ore. Titanium is very useful in aircraft, and scientists are looking for new, more efficient methods of producing it.

RECYCLING NUCLEAR FUEL

Some used uranium fuel can be reprocessed (or recycled) to reduce nuclear waste and cut costs. There are nuclear reprocessing plants in France, Russia, and the United Kingdom. They recycle about 5,500 tons (5,000 t) of used fuel per year. People who are opposed to the use of nuclear power are worried about reprocessing. They say that it is dangerous and still leaves nuclear waste that has to be stored or disposed of.

RECYCLE RECYCLE RECYCLE

Mining Metal Ore

Miners dig metallic ores from the ground all over the world. **Geologists** find new sources by test drilling to check whether there is enough of an ore to be worth mining. The tests show how deep the ore is and allow mining companies to decide which kind of mine is best. Some ore deposits are near the surface, but others may be buried deep underground.

Types of Mine

Open-pit mines recover metals from thick beds of ore that lie close to the surface. Miners use explosives to break up the surface rocks. Huge mechanical shovels then dig out the deposits and load them onto trucks. Deeper deposits are reached by digging vertical shafts. Horizontal tunnels lead off from the shafts, and miners or remote-controlled drilling equipment break chunks of ore from the rock face.

BIGGEST PITS

The Chuquicamata copper mine in northern Chile is one of the largest open pits. It is 2.7 miles (4.3 km) long, 1.9 miles (3 km) wide, and more than 930 yards (850 m) deep. It produces about 32 million tons (29 million t) of copper per year. The world's deepest iron mine is Kiruna in northern Sweden, at a depth of 1,143 yards (1,045 m). It produces about 16.5 million tons (15 million t) of ore per year.

Processing plants for smelting and refining copper at the Chuquicamata copper mine in Chile.

Processing Ore

Mined rocks go to nearby processing plants. There, the rocks are crushed and washed. Some crushed ores are mixed with liquids, so that metal particles sink to the bottom and can be separated. The ore particles are dried and often formed into round pellets, which makes them easier to ship and use.

Top Iron Producers

Country	Millions of metric tons per year	% of world total
China	588	32.6
Brazil	318	17.7
Australia	275	15.3
India	140	7.8
Russia	102	5.7
Ukraine	74	4.1
USA	53	2.9
S. Africa	41	2.3
Canada	34	1.9
Sweden	23	1.3

Biggest Maker

China is the world's biggest producer of the two most common metals, aluminum and iron (see right). Despite this, China's economy is growing so fast that it still imports more aluminum than it exports. China has produced more iron ore recently, but still imports large quantities from Australia and Brazil.

Top Aluminum Producers

Country	Millions of metric tons per year	% of world total
China	9.35	27.7
Russia	3.72	11.0
Canada	3.05	9.1
USA	2.28	6.8
Australia	1.93	5.7
Brazil	1.50	4.5
Norway	1.33	3.9
India	1.10	3.3
S. Africa	0.90	2.7
Bahrain	0.87	2.6

WHAT ABOUT THE ENVIRONMENT?

Mining damages the landscape. Digging mines creates huge holes in the ground, and land can sink when underground tunnels are excavated. Mines often dump their waste material above ground.

Today however, mining companies have to clean up after their excavations. So former mines are cleared, leveled, planted with trees and shrubs, and often turned into recreation areas.

Making Steel

We use steel to make many things, from skyscrapers to ships to saucepans. It is a hard, strong alloy of iron with carbon and small amounts of other metals, such as manganese, nickel, and tungsten. Steelmaking is an important industry in many countries of the world, and China makes more steel than any other country.

Top Steel Producers

Country	Millions of metric tons per year	% of world total
China	489.0	36.4
Japan	120.2	9.0
USA	97.2	7.2
Russia	72.2	5.4
India	53.1	4.0
South Korea	51.4	3.8
Germany	48.5	3.6
Ukraine	42.8	3.2
Brazil	33.8	2.5
Italy	32.0	2.4

How Do We Make Steel?

Steel is made from iron, which is smelted in a blast furnace. A modern steel furnace is made of steel and lined with heat-resistant bricks. Steelmakers feed in iron ore at the top, as well as coke and limestone. Blasts of hot air are blown into the lower part of the furnace. The rocky parts of the ore combine with the limestone, leaving molten iron to run off at the bottom of the blast furnace.

Molten steel pours out of a furnace at a plant using the basic oxygen process (see opposite).

Modern Methods

Manufacturers have improved on the Bessemer process (see page 9). Today, most steel is made using the basic oxygen process (BOP). First, molten iron is loaded into a furnace, along with scrap steel. A jet of oxygen blows over the molten metal inside the furnace. The oxygen combines with impurities in the metal, and these form waste slag or leave the furnace as exhaust (or waste) gases. The furnace can be tilted to pour off molten steel.

Special Steels

Steelmakers manufacture different kinds of steel by adding various alloys (see pages 16–17). They add **tungsten** and **cobalt** to harden and strengthen steel, which makes it useful for cutting tools. Galvanized steel is coated with zinc, and some steel is coated with tin to make the tinplate used for food containers. One of the most useful alloys is stainless steel, used for silverware, kitchen equipment, and surgical instruments. Steelmakers add chromium and nickel to the alloy to make stainless steel, as well as small amounts of other metals. Stainless steel is so important that it is graded in a similar way to silver. Different grades have varying amounts of various metals.

RECYCLE RECYCLE RECYCLE RECYCLE

REUSING SCRAP STEEL

BOP recycles old scrap steel to make new steel. This is similar to the way in which the ancient Romans used old copper and bronze statues (see page 7), which they considered to be scrap metal! For other ways of using scrap metal, see pages 26–27.

Mixing Metals

Most metals we use today are alloys. An alloy is a mixed metal made by combining one metal with another or with a nonmetallic substance. Bronze is an alloy made from copper and tin. Steel is an alloy made from the metal iron and the nonmetal carbon.

Metalworkers make most alloys by melting the ingredients separately and then mixing them. The mixed molten metals cool and solidify into the new alloy. Some alloys are made by mixing metal powders together and then heating them under pressure. The main reason for making alloys is to improve the properties of the metals. For example, an alloy may be harder, stronger, or more malleable than the main metal.

A worker in protective clothing pours bronze into molds to make statuettes.

Mixing Copper

Copper was used to make the world's first important alloy, bronze (see pages 6–7). Today, there are about 400 different copper alloys, including various combinations of bronze, brass, and copper-nickel-zinc mixtures.

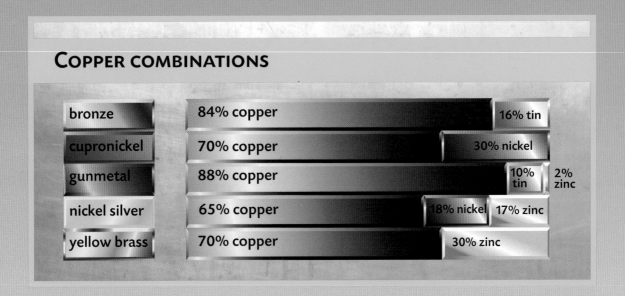

COPPER COMBINATIONS

bronze	84% copper	16% tin
cupronickel	70% copper	30% nickel
gunmetal	88% copper	10% tin / 2% zinc
nickel silver	65% copper	18% nickel / 17% zinc
yellow brass	70% copper	30% zinc

With or Without Iron?

We divide metal into two main types called ferrous and nonferrous, depending on whether or not they contain iron. Ferrous comes from the Latin word for iron, *ferrum*. Copper alloys are nonferrous. The best-known ferrous alloys are the various kinds of steel (see page 9), which combine iron with carbon. Lesser known ferrous alloys include:

- elinvar (containing iron, nickel, and chromium);
- fernico (with iron, nickel, and cobalt);
- invar (with iron and nickel);
- kovar (with iron and cobalt).

Superalloys

Some alloys can stand up to extremely high temperatures and very tough conditions without breaking, deforming, melting, or rusting. These are called superalloys. They are made mainly of nickel, cobalt, or nickel-iron mixed with chromium and other elements.

Superalloys can withstand temperatures up to 2,012°F (1,100°C). They are useful for jet engines and gas turbines used in spacecraft, planes, and ships. Many superalloys are **registered trademarks** that belong to the company that developed them. One called Inconel is mainly nickel and chromium, but also contains small quantities of aluminum, **boron**, cobalt, copper, iron, manganese, and titanium.

RECYCLE RECYCLE RECYCLE RECYCLE

SAVING RAW MATERIALS

Recycling steel saves both energy and raw materials. Recycling one metric ton of steel uses:

- 2,645 lbs. (1,200 kg) less iron ore,
- 152 lbs. (69 kg) less coal and
- 132 lbs. (60 kg) less limestone

than when we make steel using only raw materials.

Shaping Metals

Sparks fly as an oxy-fuel torch cuts through steel bars.

We shape metals when they are hot and soft. Molten metal can be poured into a hollow mold to cool, harden, and become solid. This is how we produce cast iron. Metalworkers also flatten hot metal into thin sheets between rollers, or force it through holes to make wires.

Hot Metal

Some metals have to be heated to very high temperatures before they become easy to shape. Different metals melt at different temperatures.

Metal	Melting point °F	Melting point °C	Metal	Melting point °F	Melting point °C
tungsten	6,165	3,407	copper	1,985	1,085
chromium	3,375	1,857	aluminum	1,220	660
titanium	3,020	1,660	zinc	788	420
iron	2,795	1,535	lead	622	328
uranium	2,070	1,132	tin	450	232

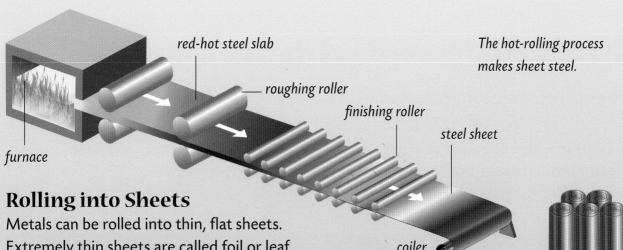

red-hot steel slab

roughing roller

finishing roller

steel sheet

furnace

coiler

The hot-rolling process makes sheet steel.

steel rolls

Rolling into Sheets

Metals can be rolled into thin, flat sheets. Extremely thin sheets are called foil or leaf (for example very thin gold leaf), and pieces thicker than ¼ inch (6 mm) are known as plate (such as thick steel plate). Steel is often rolled into sheets, and so are other metals such as aluminum, brass, copper, nickel, tin, and titanium.

To make sheet steel, manufacturers reheat thick slabs of cast steel and pass them between heavy rollers that squeeze the steel into plate. This moves on to finishing rollers, which press the metal sheets to make them even thinner. At the end of the line, a machine rolls the sheet into a coil.

Sheets of Steel

The thickness of sheet metal is called its gauge. This is measured in different units for various metals. Sheet steel gauges run from ¼ inch (6 mm) to 40 times thinner! The higher the number, the thinner the sheet.

gauge	thickness in inches (mm)	
3	0.2391 in.	(6.0731 mm)
10	0.1345 in.	(3.4163 mm)
20	0.0329 in.	(0.9119 mm)
30	0.0120 in.	(0.3048 mm)
38	0.0060 in.	(0.1524 mm)

Cutting and Joining

We can cut hard metals with even harder metals. For example, tungsten is used in the tips of high-speed metal-cutting tools. A metal can also be heated by an oxy-fuel torch, which mixes fuel with oxygen to burn through metal and cut it. The same process can be used to join metals, or **weld** them. The torch heats the metals, and the molten parts are pushed together and then allowed to cool. Electrical sparks, or arcs, can also weld metal pieces together. **Laser** beams can do the same job.

RECYCLE RECYCLE RECYCLE

REUSING LEFTOVERS

Small items, such as lids and bottle tops, are stamped from large sheets of metal such as steel. The leftover metal in the spaces between the shapes can be remelted and recycled, saving energy and materials.

Precious Metals

People prize two metals above all others: gold and silver. They became known as precious metals because they are scarce and can be used to make beautiful, shiny objects. Gold and silver became valuable trading items.

These young prospectors are panning for gold in an Australian stream.

A third precious metal called platinum was known in the ancient Americas, where it was found by invading Europeans in the sixteenth century. Scientists call gold, silver, and platinum noble metals, together with mercury. This is because they all resist chemical reactions, do not corrode easily, and keep their beauty and usefulness.

VALUABLE FOREVER

There is no problem in recycling precious metals: they are so valuable that no one wants to throw them away. They can be sold as objects or melted down for reuse. In mid-2009, silver was worth about $14, gold $945, and platinum $1,200 per troy ounce (31.1 grams).

also a high-tech metal. Gold reflects heat, light, and radiation well, so it can protect spacecraft from the sun's rays. It conducts electricity well, so gold is the best metal for small electronic contacts and switches in computers, TVs, and phones. As gold is expensive, it is usually added as a thin film on top of other metals. Very thin gold wire (measuring a hundredth of a millimeter) is used to connect electronic parts.

Precious Little

In 2006, 243 tons (221 t) of platinum were produced around the world. This is less than a tenth of the gold produced, which was itself much less than silver. Just over 22,000 tons (20,000 t) of silver were produced. This compares with nearly 37.5 million tons (34 million t) of aluminum!

Silver Compounds

Silver is best known in jewelry, as well as being used to make ornaments and silverware. Silver also plays a role in photographic film. Some silver compounds change according to the amount of light thrown on them and show up as a picture, so they are used on plastic film.

Top Ten Producers

Gold	Platinum	Silver
S. Africa	S. Africa	Peru
USA	Russia	Mexico
China	Canada	China
Australia	Zimbabwe	Australia
Peru	USA	Chile
Indonesia	Colombia	Poland
Russia	Finland	Russia
Canada	Japan	USA
Uzbekistan	Australia	Canada
Ghana	Botswana	Kazakhstan

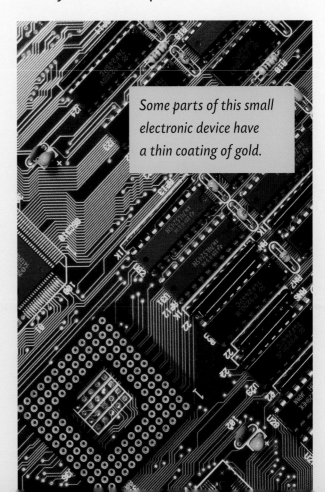

Some parts of this small electronic device have a thin coating of gold.

High-tech Beauty

Gold is best known for its beauty. People have made jewelry and valuable ornaments from gold for thousands of years. But it is

Metals for Strength and Beauty

Today we think of metals as industrial materials. Metal is used to make machinery, and metal machines produce many useful objects. But artists, designers, and craftspeople also use metals. They make jewelry from gold and silver and use other metals for buildings and sculptures.

Scraping the Skyline

Many of the skyscrapers on New York City's skyline are based on metals and have steel frames and metal decoration. The Chrysler Building was designed in 1930 in a style known as **art deco**. Its famous top section is covered in stainless steel which gives it a bright, silvery look. The Seagram Building has a steel and reinforced concrete frame covered with sheets of bronze around the large windows. This building style is called **modernist** or **international**. The Citigroup Center has a distinctive sloping roof and is covered with aluminum, a light metal which helps reduce the weight of the structure on its foundations.

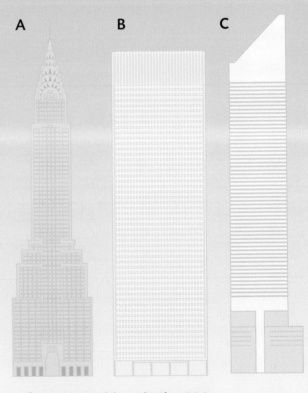

Stainless steel arches form the top section of the Chrysler Building.

A **Chrysler Building: built 1930,** 1,047 feet (319 m) tall, stainless steel

B **Seagram Building: built 1958,** 515 feet (157 m) tall, bronze

C **Citigroup Center: built 1977,** 915 feet (279 m) tall, aluminum

Bronze Casts

Bronze has always been a favorite material for sculptors, because it is easy to cast, looks good, and has a warm color and smooth texture. It also wears well and is weatherproof. One of the twentieth century's greatest sculptors made large bronze pieces. Henry Moore (1898–1986) started by making models of his pieces in plaster or clay. Then he made a mold of the model and poured molten bronze into it. He often made a small model first and then increased the size of the mold, so the finished bronze sculpture was huge.

Working in Iron

Nineteenth-century artists used iron and steel as cheap substitutes for expensive bronze. Then around 1930, sculptors began using the cheaper metals. They hammered and twisted pieces before **soldering** them

This bronze sculpture by Henry Moore is called Oval with Points.

(joining them together with a hot mixture of tin and lead). One of the century's greatest artists, Pablo Picasso (1881–1973), used these techniques. He sometimes painted his finished iron or steel pieces.

FABERGÉ'S EGGS

The Russian jeweler Peter Carl Fabergé (1846–1920) used gold, silver, and gemstones to make fabulous Easter eggs for Tsar Alexander III. Fabergé made one every year for the tsar to give to his wife, Empress Maria. Fabergé is still a luxury brand today.

Recycling Cans

Almost all metals can be recycled, and every year more than 440 million tons (400 million t) of metal are recycled around the world. The metals we recycle most are steel and aluminum, mainly because of all the cans we use.

Tin cans are not made of tin (although they were many years ago). Today, most food cans are made of tin-plated steel, and most drink cans of aluminum. These cans can be recycled easily by putting them in a recycling bin or taking them to a recycling center.

From Used to New

Used aluminum cans go to plants where machinery presses them into small **briquettes** or larger **bales**. Then they go to manufacturers. Here the pressed cans are crushed and shredded, and their labels are burned off. The small metal pieces produced are loaded into melting furnaces, where recycled metal mixes with new aluminum.

SAVING ENERGY

- Recycling 2.2 lbs. (1 kg) of aluminum saves up to 13.2 lbs. (6 kg) of bauxite, 8.8 lbs. (4 kg) of chemicals, and 14 kWh of electricity.
- Recycling aluminum uses 5% of the energy and produces 5% of the CO_2 emissions of new aluminum.
- Recycling one aluminum can saves enough energy to run a TV for three hours.
- Recycling 7 steel cans saves enough energy to power a 60-watt lightbulb for 26 hours.
- In 2006, 67.2 million tons (61 million t) of steel scrap were recycled in the U.S., and 5.5 tons (5 t) in the UK.
- The U.S. steel industry uses 29% less energy than it did in 1990.

Three green arrows make up the international recycling symbol.

Crushed cubes of used metal are ready to be recycled.

Molten metal is poured into **ingots** that are fed into rolling mills. These squeeze the metal into sheets. The sheet aluminum is coiled and sent to can manufacturers. Recycled cans can be back on supermarket shelves in just 60 days, ready to be bought, emptied, and recycled all over again. Steel cans are recycled in a similar way.

Magnetic or Not?

If aluminum and steel cans are mixed, recycling plants can separate them by using giant magnets. That's because steel is magnetic and aluminum is not.

Try holding a magnet against a can: if it is pulled to the can, the can is probably made of steel. Recyclable steel is also used to make pet-food cans, aerosol cans, household containers, cookie tins, and jam-jar lids.

Foil versus Can

Aluminum foil and cans are made of different alloys and need to be recycled separately. Bottle and jar tops, baking trays, and freezing trays can all be recycled. Metal-coated plastic film, which is often used for chips and snack bags, cannot be recycled. Use the scrunch test to check whether a package is aluminum. If it springs back when you scrunch it in your hand, you can't recycle it.

Scrap Metal

Scrap metal merchants are great recyclers. Scrap metal is valuable material, and this includes nearly all kinds of metal. Most scrap dealers sell by weight, separating metal from other materials. They buy some of their material from merchants who drive around streets looking for scrap metal. Homeowners are often happy to give them old metal objects, pleased to have them taken away.

Valuable Materials

In mid-2009 scrap tin was worth about $7 per pound. Nickel was almost half as valuable, and copper was worth about a sixth as much as tin.

Different Kinds of Scrap

There are three kinds of scrap metal. Home scrap is created when the metal is first produced at a factory, mill, or foundry. This metal can be recycled more or less immediately. Prompt scrap is the name given to the extra bits of waste when metal is made into a product, such as a washing machine. This is sold back to the

These crushed cars will soon leave the scrap yard in California for recycling.

original factory. Finally, there is obsolete scrap, which is made up of metal products at the end of their lives. This can range from a food can to a car or a steel bridge. All this scrap metal can be recycled.

Workers collect scrap metal at a ship-breaking yard on the coast of India.

Ships and Cars

Today, all metal ships and almost all cars are recycled. More than three-quarters of a car is made of metal, so this recycling is very important. There are far fewer ships than cars, but they are a big source of steel and other metals.

Today most **ship-breaking** is done in the Asian countries of Bangladesh, China, India, Pakistan, and Turkey. Between 600 and 700 ships are taken to these countries every year to be broken up for scrap. Recycling the metal is a good idea, but environmental groups say that coastlines are being ruined and low paid workers face dangers from other **hazardous materials** in the old ships.

MORE EVERY YEAR

The U.S. Steel Recycling Institute says almost all the steel in U.S. cars is recycled when they are scrapped. About nine-tenths of electrical appliances, such as washing machines, are recycled. And nearly two-thirds of steel containers, such as food cans, are recycled.

The British Metal Recycling Association says that nearly three-quarters of new lead in the UK is made from recycled lead. Half of new steel and more than a third of aluminum is made from recycled materials.

Metals in the Future

In the early twenty-first century, there is no shortage of most metals. In recent times we have begun to recycle more and more materials, including metals. But metal production still uses vast amounts of energy, and future scientists will need to develop new technologies, sources, and uses.

Steelworks, such as this one in Germany, might produce less pollution in future.

New Technologies

Making steel and other metals adds to the environmental problems facing our planet. These problems include air pollution and **global warming**, which is made worse by **greenhouse gases**. Metal industries are researching new ways of reducing the waste gases they give off when making metals. The World Steel Association has set up a CO_2 Breakthrough Program, which will try to find new steelmaking technologies that do not give off **carbon dioxide** (a greenhouse gas) or might produce less of it.

Mining asteroids

We know that many large asteroids —rocks that orbit the sun—contain metals such as iron and nickel. Scientists believe that an asteroid measuring .62 mi. (1 km) across could contain more than 2,204 million tons (2,000 million t) of iron-nickel ore. This is an enormous amount, more than the total volume we mine on Earth in a year. If iron or other metals become scarce, we could try mining in space.

Could asteroids be a future source of metals?

Strong and Transparent?

Some researchers think it might be possible to make see-through metals. A transparent steel alloy could be used instead of glass for some buildings, which would make them stronger. Scientists at a research laboratory in Germany have come up with a transparent form of aluminum oxide by heating fine-grained aluminum to 2,192°F (1,200°C). The aluminum oxide could be used to make lightweight, see-through metal in future.

Futuristic Fuel

Can you believe that the car of the future could run on metal fuel? That is what some scientists believe. To make this work, chunks of aluminum, boron, or iron will be ground into very fine powder. When the powder is burned at an extremely high temperature, it releases huge amounts of energy and very little else, so there are no waste gases to pollute the air. Metal powder is already used in some rocket engines, but we need to adapt this for safe use on our roads.

RECYCLE RECYCLE RECYCLE RECYCLE

IMPROVING THE RECYCLING RATE

Metal recycling is growing all the time and will continue to increase in the future. The World Steel Association says that the countries with the highest recycling rates for steel are:
Belgium (93 percent)
Germany (91 percent)
Japan (85 percent).
In the future, many other countries should be able to recycle at least 90 percent of the metal they use.

Glossary

alloy   A mixed metal made by combining one metal with another or others or with a nonmetallic substance.

art deco   A design style of the 1920s and 1930s that used geometric patterns and bold colors.

atom   The basic particle of all matter.

bale   A large bundle.

boron   A nonmetallic chemical element that is usually prepared as a brown powder.

briquette   A small block of pressed material.

carbon dioxide (CO_2)   A greenhouse gas given off when fossil fuels (such as coal, oil, and gas) are burned.

cobalt   A silvery white metallic element.

coke   A solid fuel made from coal.

compound   Something made by combining two or more different things, such as metals and chemicals.

ductile   Describing something that can be stretched into thin wire.

element   A substance that cannot be separated into a simpler form.

forge   To shape metal by heating and then hammering it.

furnace   An oven-like structure in which materials can be heated to very high temperatures.

generator   A machine that turns mechanical energy into electrical energy.

geologist   A scientist who studies the structure of the Earth.

global warming   Heating up of the Earth's surface, especially caused by pollution from burning fossil fuels.

greenhouse gas   A gas, such as carbon dioxide, that traps heat from the sun near Earth and helps to create the greenhouse effect.

hazardous materials   Materials that are very dangerous to living things or the environment.

impurity   An unwanted substance, such as dirt, that could lower the quality of metal.

ingot   A rectangular mold used for casting metals.

international (style)   A style of architecture in the 1930s and 1940s that used geometric shapes, large windows, and little decoration.

laser   A device that generates an intense beam of light.

malleable   Describing something that can be hammered or shaped without breaking.

modernist (style)   A style that aims to break with old-fashioned, traditional techniques.

mold   A hollow container that gives shape to a molten substance when it hardens.

nucleus   The central part of an atom.

ore   A rock or mineral containing a useful metal or valuable mineral.

precious metal   One of the valuable metals—gold, silver, or platinum.

radioactive   Describing a substance, such as uranium, that gives off energy in the form of streams of particles.

registered trademark   A name or symbol for a product or company that is officially recorded and cannot be copied.

ship-breaking   Breaking up old ships for scrap.

smelting   Heating and melting ore in order to get metal from it.

solder   To join metals together with a hot mixture of tin and lead.

tungsten   A hard gray metal with a very high melting point.

weld   To join metals together by heating them until they melt and pressing or hammering them together.

Web Sites

A short history of metals and metalworking.
http://neon.mems.cmu.edu/cramb/Processing/history.html

An explanation of the chemistry of metals.
www.chem4kids.com/files/elem_metal.html

Information and statistics from the British Metals Recycling Association.
www.recyclemetals.org

Facts, activity sheets, videos, and lots more on steel from the North American Steel Recycling Institute (SRI).
http://recycle-steel.org

Fun facts and interactive pages from the SRI and Roscoe (Recycle Our Steel, Conserve Our Environment).
www.recycleroom.org

A wide-ranging A–Z glossary of metals terms.
http://metals.about.com/cs/governmentdata/l/blglossary_a.htm

Index